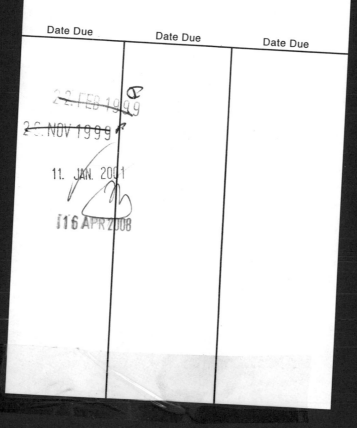

CIRCUS

CHARLES SULLIVAN

An ADVENTURES IN ART Book

RIZZOLI
NEW YORK

What is the Circus?

Once upon a time I went
way inside a circus tent,
and saw so much that I can't say
exactly what you'll find today,
but here
      (if you would like to see)
            is what the circus means to me!

Henri Matisse (1869–1954). French painter, sculptor,
and printmaker, whose joyful book, *Jazz* (1947), was
based on vivid memories of the circus and other
delights of his early life.

The Circus by Henri Matisse, 1947

The Circus is Colors

Do you want a surprise?
Close both of your eyes
until I tell you when,
and you will see the colors
of high-flying women and men,
of horses, tigers, and elephants
and acrobats, and then
the funny clowns
going 'round and 'round
as the circus starts again!

Albina Kosiec Felski (Born 1916).
Canadian who moved to Chicago and
worked in an electronics factory for
twenty-seven years while she became a
folk artist. Her detailed, colorful pictures
of animals are increasingly popular.

The Circus by Albina Kosiec Felski, 1971

The Circus is Popcorn

When I hear popcorn POP! POP! POP!
I wish that it would never stop,
so every hungry clown I meet
could catch it all and EAT! EAT! EAT!

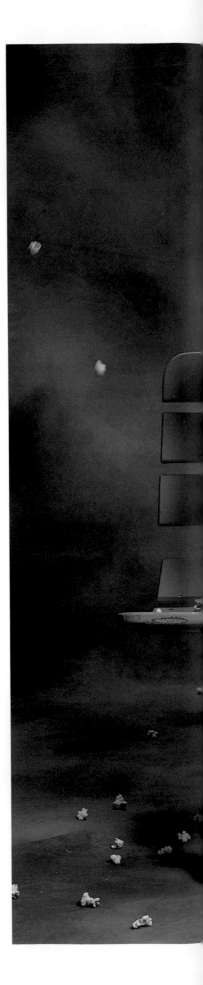

David Larible and a young friend
enjoy popcorn at the circus.
Photograph from Ringling Brothers
and Barnum & Bailey Circus

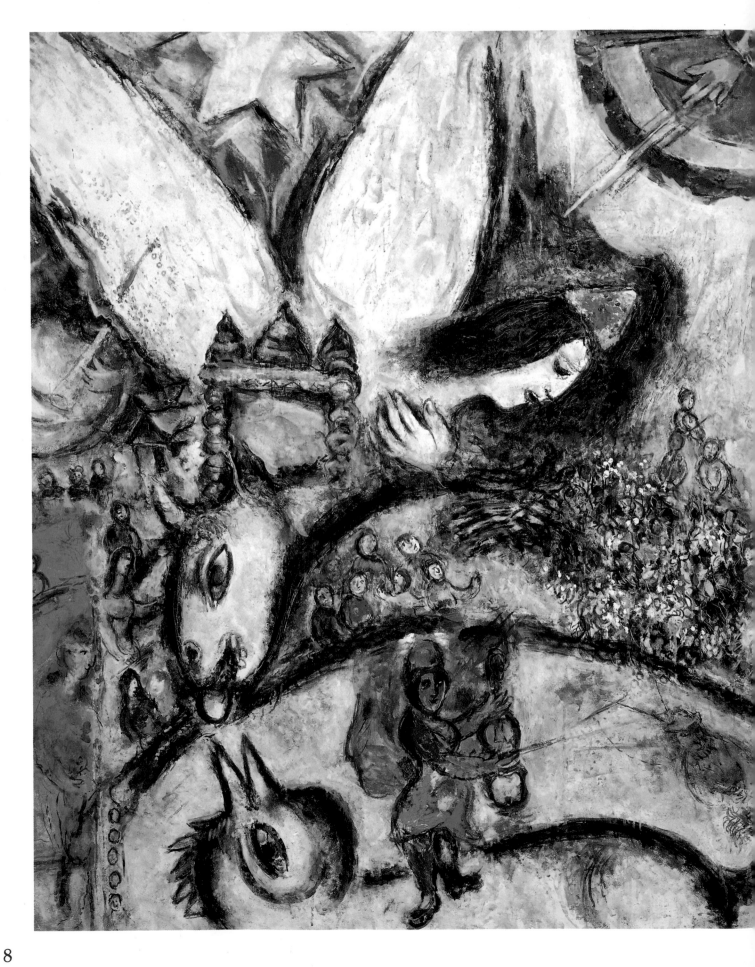

The Circus is Mystery

The beautiful star of the circus
has taken a graceful bow;
now she will climb
higher
and higher,
and walk through the air
on a thin silver wire,
but we will be wondering how?

The Big Circus by
Marc Chagall, 1968

Marc Chagall (1887–1985). Early
modern artist, born in Russia, whose
circus scenes are among the most
exciting and mysterious pictures he
painted after moving to France.

The Circus is Animals

At the circus once,
I saw a trainer
riding a "big cat,"
so I tried to ride
my cat like that,
and she scratched me
where I sat!

Gunther Gebel-Williams, the great animal
trainer, with one of his beloved tigers.
Photograph from Ringling Brothers and
Barnum & Bailey Circus

The Circus is Music

Let's join the circus
and play with the band,
song after song
all day long.

Isn't it fun
when the show has begun
to pretend we belong?

Clowns make music at the circus.
Photograph from Ringling Brothers
and Barnum & Bailey Circus

13

Lion and cage from *Circus* by
Alexander Calder, 1926–1931

14

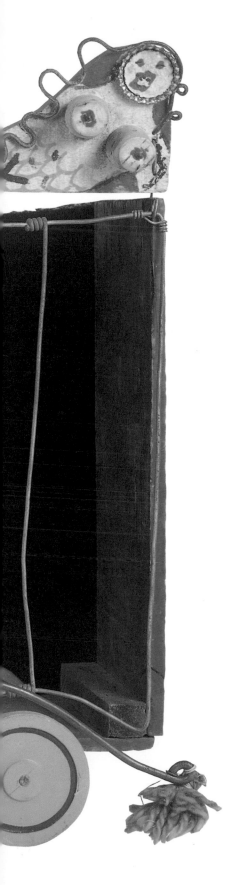

The Circus is Wagons

Some toys
make noise,
but which would make more fuss—
a lion in a wagon
or a dragon on the bus?

Alexander Calder (1898–1976). American
artist who created a complete circus made of
wire, cloth, and other materials; he liked it so
much that he often played with it himself.

The Circus by Charles Demuth, 1917

The Circus is Acrobats

Last night I dreamed of riding
a circus horse like that—
but I jumped out of bed
and bumped my head—
I won't be an acrobat.

Charles Demuth (1883–1935).
American artist whose distin-
guished watercolors include
lively scenes of circus performers
and other entertainers in action.

The Circus is Clowns

Some clowns eat nothing
but pink cotton candy,
some like to dress up as Raggedy Andy,
others would rather be Raggedy Ann,
and one is a "Granny"
who's really a man!

Barry Lubin as "Grandma" in the Big Apple Circus, New York.
Photograph by Patricia Lanza

Could I be a Clown?

You're still too young to be a clown,

and sometimes you're too serious,

but when the circus comes to town,

I bet you'll be delirious!

Pablo Picasso (1881–1973). Spanish artist,
enormously talented and influential in
painting, sculpture, and other fields,
who lived mostly in France. He often
portrayed friends and relatives, such as
his son Paul.

Paul as Harlequin
by Pablo Picasso, 1924

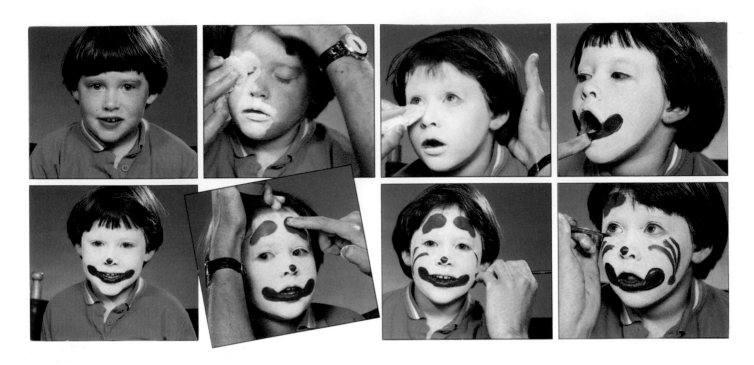

Photographs by Doug Peck, from the Klutz Press, Palo Alto, CA.

A clown is what I'd like to be,
and so my teacher's painting me;
when I've become a funny creature
and he can't see a single feature,
I'll turn around and paint my teacher!

My hair is covered by a wig,
my nose and mouth look very big—
can anybody ever see
the clown behind this face
is me?

Jill Krementz (Born 1940). American photographer and author, whose numerous eye-catching books include *A Very Young Gymnast* (1978) and *A Very Young Circus Flyer* (1979).

One of my friends

was a happy clown

who let me watch him

put his costume on:

big lips, big nose,

weird hair, and sloppy clothes,

and worn out shoes with

floppy

toes.

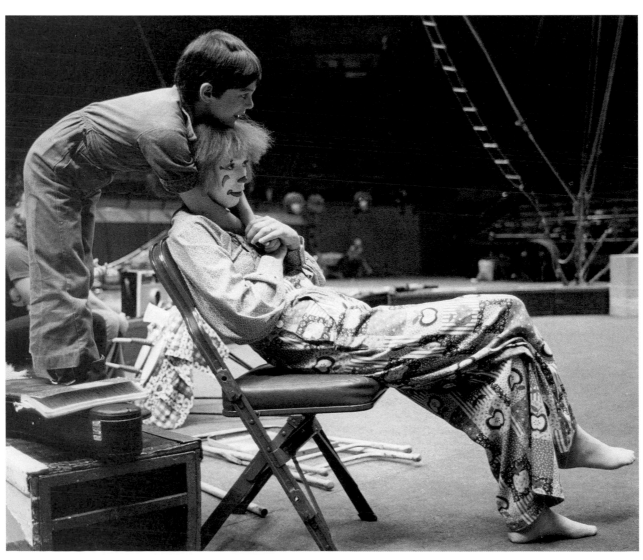

Photographs by Jill Krementz

It's a Struggle to Juggle

It's a struggle to juggle—

first

 to throw all of the balls in the air,

and then

 to keep them there!

Two Little Circus Girls by
Pierre Auguste Renoir, 1879

Pierre Auguste Renoir (1841–1919).
French impressionist who celebrated
life through his warm, charming
paintings of girls and women, as well
as still lifes and exuberant landscapes.

"I'll show you how to juggle,"
said a very clever clown:
"Throw one thing quickly in the air
while two are coming down!"

Huel Speight shows that practice
makes perfect juggling.
Photograph from Ringling Brothers
and Barnum & Bailey Circus

28

Learning to Fly with Horses

Once I saw a rider

who could stand on a horse's back,

and then—with people clapping—

she would *fly* around the track!

The Circus by
Georges Seurat, 1891

Georges Seurat (1859–1891). French artist
whose scientific interest in human vision led
him to "Pointillism," using many small points
of colored paint to produce delightful pictures.

The rider is full of pride
when she can sit astride,
and straddle this big horse
without a saddle.

Sarakoul Tchalabaeva from
Kazakhstan. Photograph from
Ringling Brothers and Barnum &
Bailey Circus

A circus horse
must learn a lot
before his trainer
lets him trot
around the ring,
or start to practice
cantering.

Henri de Toulouse-Lautrec (1864–1901). French
aristocrat who explored the world of entertainment,
immortalizing some of its characters through his
masterful paintings, prints, and posters.

In the Circus Fernando: The Ringmaster
by Henri de Toulouse-Lautrec, 1888

At the Circus: Horse Rearing
by Henri de Toulouse-Lautrec, 1899

What Can Monkeys and Chimps Do?

When I was six,
or maybe a bit older,
I wished that a little monkey
would climb on my shoulder
and do tricks.

Georges Rouault (1871–1958). French
artist known for powerful expressionistic
paintings that include the strong black
outlines he learned to draw as an
apprentice to a stained-glass maker.

Clown and Monkey
by Georges Rouault, 1910

Monkeys are funky,
and some play the blues,
but for real circus music
the chimps I would choose!

Chimpanzees play jazz at the circus.
Photograph from Ringling Brothers
and Barnum & Bailey Circus

Elephants Can Do Almost Anything!

Cyrk is the word for circus

in Poland, far away,

but *work* is what this elephant does,

although it looks like play!

Waldemar Swierzy (Born 1931). Polish graphic artist and teacher, whose award-winning posters and prints have been featured at major shows in Europe and Latin America.

Polish circus poster by
Waldemar Swierzy, 1972

Wouldn't it be a treat
to stand on your hands
and *flip*!
and land on your feet?

David Hockney (Born
1937). British artist
who moved to the
United States. His
bold, innovative work
includes paintings,
photographic collages,
and theatrical set
designs.

Harlequin by
David Hockney,
1980

42

Elephants can walk
on four legs or two
(just like you)
or stand on their heads
instead.

An elephant does a
very large headstand.
Photograph from
Ringling Brothers and
Barnum & Bailey
Circus

Elephants on parade. Photograph from
Ringling Brothers and Barnum & Bailey
Circus

THIS IS THE CIRCUS!

AUTHOR'S NOTE

When I was a child, my family often moved from one place to another, but somehow we got to Boston or New York every year to see the circus. I can still remember the thrill of arriving at Madison Square Garden, finding our seats, trying to look everywhere at once, tasting the popcorn and cotton candy, smelling the unmistakable circus smells, hearing the noise, and then the loud voice of the ringmaster saying: "Ladies and Gentlemen, . . ." when the circus was about to begin. He didn't say "children" or "kids," but in fact the place was full of children, accompanied by grown-ups and excited about the great show that was spread out before them.

A year ago I took my grandson Frank and his parents to see the circus near Washington, and through him I began to relive my old memories of elephants and clowns, acrobats and bareback riders, all kinds of animals, colors, and sounds, moments of suspense and moments of mystery. Frank (not yet three years old) stood most of the time, his chin on a lower railing, completely fascinated by what was going on. Soon after that wonderful experience, I decided to create this book so that more of today's children (and grown-ups) could enjoy the adventures of the circus as I and my family have done. Frank may be a circus fan for life!

This is the first of a series of books. I am calling them ADVENTURES IN ART because each of them will invite young people to learn about an interesting, exciting subject, such as the world of the circus, using paintings, drawings, photographs, and other works of art as illustrations. I will be delighted if these books are enjoyed again and again, until they become worn and much-loved old favorites. So please write to me about *Circus*. Do you like it? What do you like best? Is there anything about it that you don't like? (My address: Post Office Box 1775, Annapolis, MD 21404.)

I dedicate this book to Frank, his brother Edward, and circus-lovers everywhere! And a special note of thanks to my editor, Lois Brown.

CHARLES SULLIVAN
Washington D.C.

ACKNOWLEDGMENTS

Alexander Calder. *Lion and Cage* from *Calder's Circus*, 1926–1931. Lion: Wire, yarn, cloth and button. Cage: painted wood, wire, cloth, cork and bottle caps. Dimensions: lion: 9½ x 16½ x 5". Cage: 17⅛ x 19½ x 17½". Collection of Whitney Museum of American Art. Purchase; a public fundraising campaign May 1982, additional funds by the Robert Wood Johnson Jr. Charitable Trust, The Lauder Foundation; Robert Lehman Foundation, Inc.; Howard and Jean Lipman Foundation Inc.; anonymous donor; T.M. Evans Foundation, Inc.; MacAndrews & Forbes Group, Inc.; De Witt Wallace Fund, Inc.; Martin and Agneta Gruss; Anne Phillips; Mr. and Mrs. Laurance S. Rockefeller; Simon Foundation, Inc.; Marylou Whitney; Bankers Trust Co.; Mr. and Mrs. Kenneth N. Dayton; Joel and Anne Ehrenkranz; Irvin and Kenneth Feld; Flora Whitney Miller, and more than 500 individuals. 83.36.36a-b

Marc Chagall. *Le Grand Cirque* (The Big Circus), 1968. Oil on canvas, 67 x 63". Private Collection. Copyright © A.D.A.G.P.

Charles Demuth, *The Circus*, 1917. Columbus Museum of Art, Ohio. Gift of Ferndinand Howald.

Albina Kosiec Felski. *The Circus*, 1971. Acrylic on canvas, 48 x 48¼". National Museum of American Art, Smithsonian Institution, Gift of Herbert Waide Hemphill, Jr., and Museum purchase made possible by Ralph Cross Johnson. 1986.65.108

David Hockney. *Harlequin*, 1980. Oil on canvas. 48 x 36". Copyright © David Hockney.

Jill Krementz. Photographs from *A Very Young Circus Flyer*. Dell Publishing Co. Inc. Copyright © 1979 Jill Krementz.

Patricia Lanza. Photograph of "Grandma" (Barry Lubin) of the Big Apple Circus, New York.

Henri Matisse. *Le Cirque* (The Circus), published 1947. Color stencil in gouache, plate II from "Jazz" (Tiriade Publishers, Paris, 1944–1947). National Gallery of Art, Washington. Gift of Mr. and Mrs. Andrew S. Keck.

Doug Peck. Photographs from *FacePainting*. Copyright © The Klutz Press, Palo Alto, CA.

Pablo Picasso. *Paul en Arlequin* (Paul as Harlequin), 1924. Musée Picasso. Photograph © R.M.N.

Pierre Auguste Renoir. *Two Little Circus Girls*, 1878–79. Oil on canvas, 131.5 x 99.5 cm. Art Institue of Chicago Potter Palmer Collection.

Photographs on pages: 6–7, 11, 12–13, 29, 32–33, 38, 43, 44–45, courtesy of Ringling Brothers and Barnum & Bailey Combined Shows Inc.

Georges Rouault. *Clown and Monkey*, 1910. Monotype, printed in color, plate: 22⅝ x 14¼". Collection, The Museum of Modern Art, New York. Gift of Mrs. Sam A. Lewisohn.

Georges Seurat. *Le Cirque* (The Circus), 1891. Musée d'Orsay. Photograph copyright © R.M.N.

Waldemar Swierzy. Polish Circus Poster, 1972. Lithograph. Prints and Photographs Division, Library of Congress, Washington.

Henri de Toulouse-Lautrec. *Au Cirque: Cheval Pointant* (At the Circus: Horse Rearing), 1899. Black chalk with red and yellow chalk. The Fine Arts Museums of San Francisco, Achenback Foundation for Graphic Arts, Elizabeth Ebert and Arthur W. Barney Fund. 1977.2.5

Henri de Toulouse-Lautrec. *In the Circus Fernando: The Ringmaster,* 1887–88. Oil on canvas, 100.3 x 161.3 cm. Copyright © 1992 Art Institute of Chicago. Joseph Winterbotham Collection.

First published in the United States of America in 1992 by
RIZZOLI INTERNATIONAL PUBLICATIONS, INC.
300 Park Avenue South, New York, N.Y. 10010

Library of Congress Cataloging in Publication Data

Sullivan, Charles, 1933–
    Circus / Charles Sullivan.
        p.   cm. — (An Adventures in Art Book)
    Summary: Presents poems about the circus
illustrated with paintings by such artists as Toulouse-
Lautrec, Marc Chagall, and Alexander Calder, and
photographs from the Ringling Brothers and Big Apple
circuses.
    ISBN 0-8478-1604-4
    1. Circus—Juvenile poetry.   2. Circus in art—Juvenile
literature.   3. Children's poetry, American.   [1. Circus—
Poetry.   2. Circus in art.   3. American poetry.]   I. Title.
II. Series.
PS3569.U345C57   1992
811'.54—dc20   9219430
                                                                    CIP
                                                                    AC

Design: Gilda Hannah

Printed in Singapore